Rapt in Reverie

Kishori Mahadik

BookLeaf
Publishing

India | USA | UK

Dedication

To Leopold, 'wink'

Since we've both been single for a while,

we should definitely get together.

Acknowledgements

I am indebted to Samudra and Sindhu for being my pillars of strength and motivating me to pursue my dreams. Thank you to my dear friend and cheerleader, Seetha. Her encouragement and support have been invaluable in developing my ideas. I am immensely grateful to Dr. Pacchi for recognising my writing talent at a young age. I appreciate my awesome friends Deepa and Sagar! They've been so helpful by taking the time to read my poems and offering their honest feedback and helpful suggestions. Their support means the world to me! I am beyond thrilled to extend my deepest gratitude to BookLeaf Publishing for turning my dreams into reality. Here's to many more literary adventures together!

Preface

Since my school days, I've aspired to publish a book of poems. I wanted the world to see things from my perspective. I was unsure about where to begin, though. Life got busier, and this dream faded into the forgotten corners of my mind. This year, I confidently plunged in after stumbling upon a compelling Instagram reel by BookLeaf Publishing that echoed the idea I had been mulling over. It was my birthday gift to myself. It's a unique gift because it's something I always wanted and will bring me pride in the future. My poems may stick to something other than traditional rhythms and flows, but they get you thinking. Unconventional rhymes are beautiful because they can surprise and make you think. I hope you will derive as much pleasure from reading my poems as I did from composing them.

Ambition

My ambition is to achieve something that
money cannot buy,
Something that people will talk about long
after I die.
I want my life to be free and peaceful,
Just like me, astute but not deceitful.
I want to empower myself with an important
thing called choice,
Irrespective of being a woman, I give my
opinions a voice.

My ambition is to reach such a state of calm,
Where my mind won't raise an alarm or my
body does not fear any harm.
I want my life to be full of happiness and
cheer,
But when sad, someone close to lend an ear.
I want to empower myself with something as
essential as courage,
Because life teaches us lessons but does not
always encourage.

My ambition is to be able to savour the fruits of my labour,
Be bold enough to experience and enjoy life's flavour.
I want a life that is abundant and mysterious,
My health is prospering, and my mind is curious.
I want to empower myself to fulfil my dream,
It's something different but not extreme.

Smile

When a sincere yet simple smile is given to a
dear friend,
It can magically his or her heart mend.
A warm smile can make someone's heart melt.
Lighten one's mood when truly felt.
A naughty smile with a twinkle in the eye,
Express more than what words can signify.

A smile can give immense courage to a loved
one.
Banish the darkness from one's life, like the
mighty sun.
A smile can hide enigmatic emotions way too
many,
It's a special bounty but costs not a single
penny.
A smile can make one fall in love.
It's as mystical and pure as a dove.

A smile can mean you are happy from within.
Accompanied by a happy dance, a twirl or a
spin.

Funny how a smile can convey so many
things,
Brighten up a day, pure joy it surely brings.
Smile more often and let your heart sing.
Fill your life with contentment, and peace of
mind may it bring.

Wealth

When would you say that you have truly
made it?
Would it look like Scrooge McDuck, where
you could plunge into it?
Our society at large has a definition and
somehow has it quantified.
The lengths people are ready to go to achieve
it has me horrified.

Wealth is something that liberates you.
Elevate experiences or pull you through.
Wealth is health you ignore and take so
lightly.
Friends that surround you and help you
improve slightly.

Wealth lets you subtly show that you have
arrived.
Many hardships and adversities you have
survived.
Wealth lets you enjoy the finer things in life.
Appreciate things in a whole new light.

When you have amassed something tangible,
You can genuinely enjoy things that are not
quantifiable.
Wealth is something that goes beyond the
obvious.
If blessed with it, be grateful for the
bounteous.

Killer in Disguise

Every day and night, you fooled me by saying,
'You are precious to me'.
Your fake feelings and words are crystal clear;
now I can see.
You merrily wander with fair damsels, not
one, I guess more than four,
As I can see now, you don't feel my need
anymore.
I never thought that a boy like you would
turn out so bad.
The sooner I found out, the more I became
glad.

What I thought to be my mate, my lover, was
merely a killer in disguise.
Who killed my spirit of love with those
innocent eyes and tonnes of lies.
Beware! Be aware, alert and scared, as he can
be anywhere.
He'll pretend to be in love with you, then
suddenly vanish in thin air.
With him, you've got to be brave; you've got
to be wise.

If not, with him loose, one has to pay a heavy price.

Hope

Hope keeps one afloat when everything
around seems to be going down.
It can be like the light at the end of a tunnel,
with only darkness around.
Hope is a powerful saviour; it gives us a
reason to stay alive.
No matter how agonising the pain is, our
hearts will survive.
Life can disappoint, and people may betray.
Yet, hope will always have something positive
to say.
Await with confidence and infuse your life
with joy.
Pessimism and anxiety, may it destroy.

Hope gives assurance that you will get all that
you desire.
Patience and self-belief are all that you
require.
Mobilise your energy to do something good,
Our need for inner peace is often
misunderstood.

Sometimes it's something you give to a friend in need.
When they are feeling low, you should take the lead.
Hope whispers to us: Yes, it is possible.
It liberates us from our shackles, making us unstoppable.

Strong Women

'Why isn't "woman" seen as a synonym for
"strong"'?
Sadly, she has been taken for granted
overlong.
At work for some, she is a source of
inspiration.
But her success is often a topic of speculation.

'Why isn't "woman" seen as a synonym for
"brave"'?
She confidently takes charge and perseveres
when others are ready to cave.
She is seen by many only as a caretaker and
not a provider.
A few want to be like her, but the rest
secretly dislike her.

Why are women brought down with nasty
schemes?
Society is notorious for clipping her wings
and stifling her dreams.
Women with high standards are often
considered cold.

Only when opinions are voiced out are they
seen as bold.

All you strong women out there who are
unsung heroes,
You have accomplished so much because of
the paths you chose.
Kudos to you for sticking on and not giving
up hope.
Help other divas recover and find ways to
cope.

My Heart Ponders

Wondered, whether I would find you,
Wondered, whether my dreams would come
true.
All I wished to get was someone like you,
To make times happier and get rid of the
blues.

Like a warrior, you've always been brave,
In times of sorrow, you've always stayed.
You're full of things for which I have always
craved,
Only for you are all these feelings I've within
me saved.

Without you, this heart cannot stay for a
single day.
A moment passes like an hour when you're far
away.
This trust that lies between us two,
Has become like a part of me and you.

Being with you has made me realise,

How life plays games and fills you with
surprise.
Joys and sorrows are yet to come,
As our bodies two and one soul become.

Like an enigma, you came into my life,
To make things work, we both shall strive.
Love and faith we must always keep,
Only then shall we stay together in a
relationship so deep.

Work out

A relationship can work out when two people
want to stay together,
Promise to work on their flaws and love each
other forever.
Life is not very complicated; everything
eventually works out.
What you were seeking outside was always
within, as it turns out.

An invigorating rush surges to your brain
right after a workout.
Gloominess and tonnes of calories it will
burn out.
Good health and mental well-being need
daily workouts.
It will keep depression at bay and drive away
any self-doubts.

Mathematics does not help you work out your
daily problems,
Though it can help collocate your inner
thoughts in rows and columns.

Do not worry about the result; carry out your plan.
God never burdens you with things more than you can.

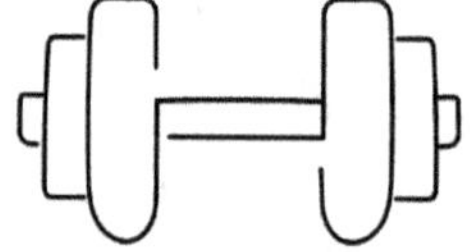

Fling

At first, it was meant to be just a fling.
Silencing the heart and letting the brain
think.
It was something we both enjoyed and
wanted.
But then we spoke, got to know each other,
and bonded.

I kept my distance because I was afraid it
would lead to something deeper.
You never expressed it with words. When I
saw it in your eyes, it made me a believer.
Even though you never say it, I know you
seriously care.
Secretly, you observe me, but you never stare.

It's not the act but the emotion that matters
to me.
We were exploring each other's bodies and
setting our minds free.
Your touch can set my core on fire.

Yet your soft kisses and warm hugs are what I
desire.

Your words inspire and resonate with
something deep within me.
If only how much you mean to me, you could
see.
It started with something raw and urgent:
passion and pleasure.
But now it is meaningful, special and
something I treasure.

Age

Age is relative; it can signify the end for some
while the beginning for others.
We realise someone's situation is not always as
it appears.
We had grand plans to age gracefully, but
naturally, life doesn't always go as planned.
We land up in situations that teach bitter life
lessons firsthand.

As we age, we cherish our past and get
anxious about our future.
Like fine wine, our spouse may appear more
refined and a bit cuter.
We wonder about how things will be; we
worry if our efforts are enough.
We will have to make choices that may be
difficult, some even tough.

As we age, we realise it has nothing to do
with numbers.
It's a mindset and how well we bounce back
from our blunders.

Trust me when I say you are as old as you
feel.
You realise only the little things are the real
deal.

As we age, we reflect on how to avoid
repeating the same mistakes our parents
made.
When life feels difficult, places with our
younger selves we want to trade.
We have reached an age where others'
opinions are irrelevant.
Be true to yourself and be confident in your
element.

Bittersweet Moment

It's unbelievable how quickly a year has flown
by!
Only in my private moments can I sigh.
Wonder if it meant anything to you; do you
secretly think about it?
All alone in my room, consumed in my
sorrows, I often do sit.

It was a bittersweet moment if only you could
see,
It brought both immense joy and deep
sadness to me.
God blessed me with something I have always
wanted,
My foolishness cost me everything, and now
my nights are haunted.

That very moment was when my whole world
came crashing down and crumbled into
pieces.
When something like this happens, your will
to live slowly decreases.

That very moment was when I felt
honest-to-goodness happiness and pure
ecstasy.
Every single step, every fleeting flashback and
every precious moment felt like an
enchanting fantasy.

At that very moment, I wanted to disappear
and never come back.
What that did to me, my love, you just cannot
track.
At that very moment, I had countless reasons
to live.
Undying love and limitless care to give.

As the days went by, I got ample time for
healing and grieving.
It has become the source of my strength and a
reason for my being.
As the days went by, I got ample time to
dream again and blossom.
It has become a reason to be brave, confident
and awesome!

Happiness

Happiness is something that cannot be
measured or compared.
The true meaning of it is yet to be declared.
It means a feeling you get from obtaining
something material.
It could be the joy you get from an experience
surreal.

It echoes not having to do chores on a Sunday
morning.
Enjoying a hot cup of chocolate when heavy
rains are pouring.
When your lover surprises you, that's when
happiness shines through.
It could mean that in your partner, you have
finally found love that is true.

Stumbling upon happiness is like finding
money in your old jeans pocket.
Reminiscing secret rendezvous while toying
with your favourite locket.
Happiness is when you have accomplished
something significant.

or celebrate the success of a friend as if you
are an essential part of it.

Planning a vacay with friends brings pure
happiness.
It's a slow weekday filled with well-deserved
laziness.
Happiness is something that cannot be
bought,
It's something fleeting and so desperately
sought.

Fear

Fear is the chill that runs down your spine
when you face your innermost dread.
When actually, it's an irrational shadow that
only exists in your head.
Its grip is so tight that you cannot fight nor
deny its might.
It clouds your judgement, blurring wrong
from right.

Fear reveals how deeply someone matters to
you.
The thought of losing them conjures scenarios
untrue.
It can lead you to actions you'd never pursue,
Only their whispered assurances and genuine
love can truly rescue.

Fear springs from the depths of your
insecurities and doubt.
You think you're an imposter, and your act
has been found out.
When in reality, you are enough and truly one
of a kind,

With boundless courage, remarkable talent
and a powerful mind.

Breathe

Do not lose yourself amidst daily life's strife.
Never feel pressured about your way of life.
Take a moment and simply breathe.
Indulge in things that make you happy, but be
discreet.

Be ready to conquer whatever life throws at
you.
You only grow stronger after what you go
through.
Do not forget to breathe, unwind and let go.
If only I had known then what I now know.

Do not be in a hurry, as nature never does
rush.
Strive to be kind, flash a smile and allow a
hint of blush.
Pamper yourself more often; luxuriate in
self-love.
You are the most important, and nobody is
above.

Whatever belongs to you will come your way.

Be grateful; your newfound joy is here to
stay.
Do not envy others; accept your fate.
Believe in your prayers because God is great.

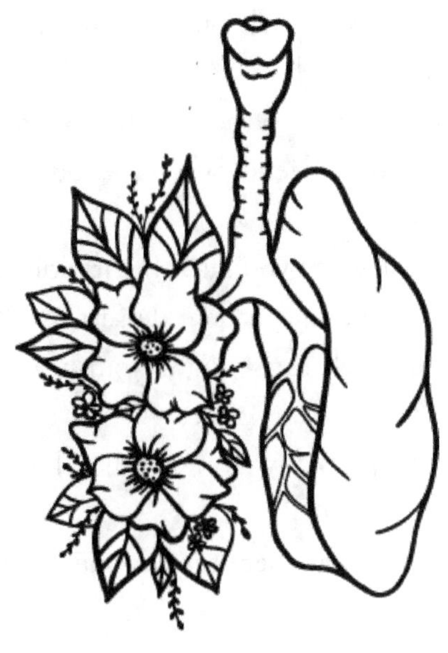

Comfort

Comfort is the feeling you experience when
you are finally home after a long day.
It is something that money can buy, but only
if done the right way.
Do not wallow in self-pity despite what you
are going through.
Draw comfort from the fact that you are
surrounded by friends who love you.

Comfort is when you take the first bite of a
cheesy pizza or a decadent dessert.
It feels insanely satisfying in your heart and
tummy without any effort.
When you plop down on your hotel bed, it
feels like a cloud.
You want to stay there forever and maybe
merrily hum aloud.

Comfort means feeling like a snug burrito on
a chilly winter night.
Feeling nostalgic after listening to music
surrounded by dim light.

Slipping into your cosy jammies, the ones you bought for a song,
It is a feeling you experience when you are somewhere you belong.

Destiny

When we met for the first time, our paths
were not aligned.
Words were left unspoken; our spark was left
behind.
Deep down, I often think about what could
have been.
Wishing I had dared to love, and let our story
begin.

I pretended like you didn't mean anything at
all.
Did this on purpose, fearing you would stall.
Terrified of getting my heart broken and
enduring the pain.
I kept my distance, even though it drove me
insane.

Trust in the rhythm of time; let your heart
sway.
Destiny will guide you on the right way.
Despite difficulties, love always finds its way.
Through life's meandering roads come what
may.

Years may go by, and seasons may change.
Our destined hearts will rearrange.
Eventually, you will come to see
that what is meant to be will always be.

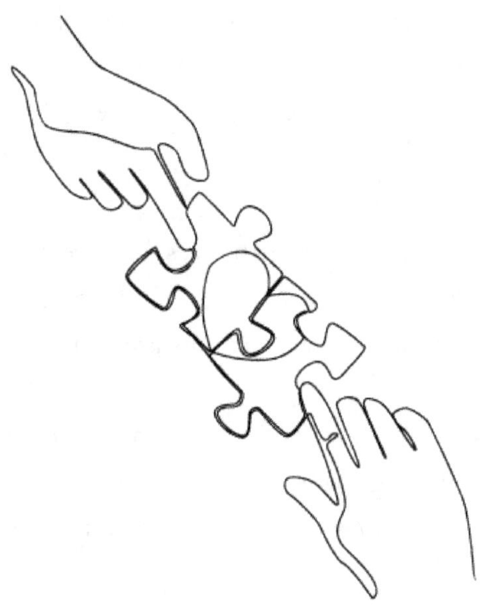

Missed Chances

We often regret the chances we didn't take
and prefer to play it safe.
Abandoning an idea or person strictly to save
face.
Why can't we be true to ourselves and take
the leap of faith?
Save the person from heartbreak and lay it
out straight.

There are no missed chances. You are never
too late,
Good things take time; they are worth the
wait.
Maybe you were ready for them, but they
needed to grow for you.
A diamond becomes a gem only after what it
goes through.

Missed chances are more than just the regrets
of lovers.
Successful people have their demons hiding
undercover.

Do not fall prey to the façade of effortless
success.
Struggles and suffering, rarely someone would
confess.

We keep yearning for what could have been.
Living in the past, sulking from within.
You are the author of your destiny.
Strive relentlessly and unlock the magic with
'open sesame'.

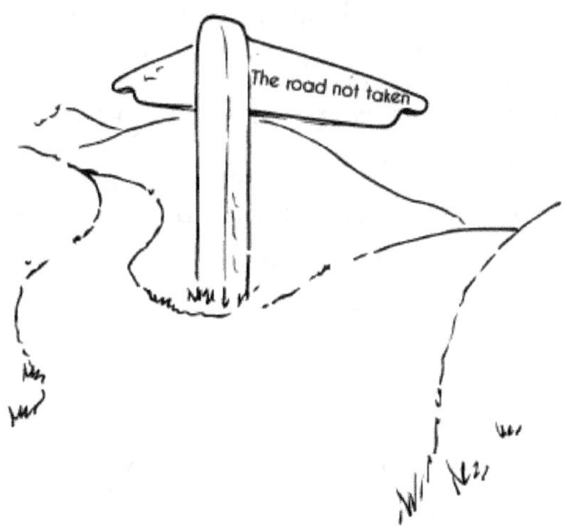

35

Rain

Tiny droplets of hope, love and blessings fall
from the sky.
The roaring sound of clouds from above, Oh!
So high;
The rains are here, so drench in your
memories and soak in their joy.
Let your spirits be high and the rains your
sorrows completely destroy.

The rains bring along black clouds with
linings of silver.
Urging you to hang on, aspire, aim and
deliver;
Couples wait eagerly for the descent of this
magical water from above.
Single souls in this weather wish they had
somebody to love.

Rains fill me with emotions that words
cannot express.
All I want is for him to cuddle and gently
caress.
Staying apart from him makes me blue.

Wish we could meet and our secret moments renew.

This distance feels even more when the rain begins to pour.
His voice, face and memories are ingrained in my core;
Feelings like these are associated with the rain,
Time goes by, but memories aplenty remain.

Best Friends

Best friends are the family you choose but are not born with.
Blood is thicker than water; it is merely a myth.
Keep them safe in your heart as you go along.
The more you put into it, the more it will grow strong.

They stick around through thick and thin,
They make you feel wanted and happy from within.
They love you dearly and make sure you are alright.
They are brutally honest with you despite being polite.

They encourage growth and celebrate success.
They forbid indulging in bad habits even under stress.
They may laugh at you when you goof around,
They shield and support you as if they were bound.

Friends will tease and mess around, but your secrets are safe with them.
If somebody tries to bring you down, they will unleash deadly mayhem.
You only have disagreements and mini-fights with your best friends.
Regardless of the gravity of the issue, your bond will never end.

Gratitude

God's blessings fill one with love and
gratitude.
Appreciating your blessings increases their
magnitude.
What you have now is what you once wanted.
You toiled for them, and so they were
granted.
Everyone wants to be valued and given thanks
freely.
They want to know you appreciate their
efforts wholeheartedly.

Value the love and support from your loved
ones.
Joy comes to those who are grateful all at
once.
Gratitude is a low-key happiness generator.
Your wishes come true sooner than later.
Make someone happy, and it will come back.
You may forget, but God is keeping track.

Tomorrowland

Tomorrowland is the promised land for EDM lovers.
It is a whole new experience that one discovers.
Music buffs swarm there for bangers and to take in the vibe.
To dance, get together and revel with their tribe.

It is a magical place where time stands still.
Your mind and body permeate with euphoria and thrill.
Memories galore and a flood of emotions will fill your heart.
At the end of the festival, you won't want to part.

www.ingramcontent.com/pod-product-compliance
Lightning Source LLC
LaVergne TN
LVHW021304200726
843509LV00012B/1770